SMALL BUTTERFLY

Copyright 2017

Printed in The U.S.A.

All right reserved. This Coloring books or any potion thereof many not be reproduced or used in any manner whatsoever without the exoress written permission of the publisher except.

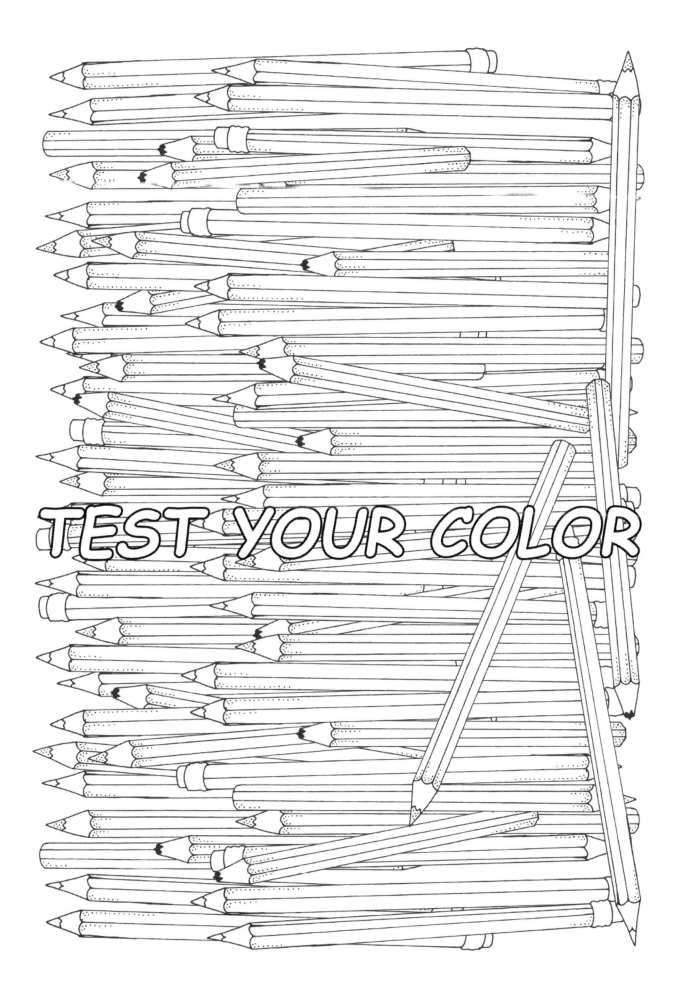

1.

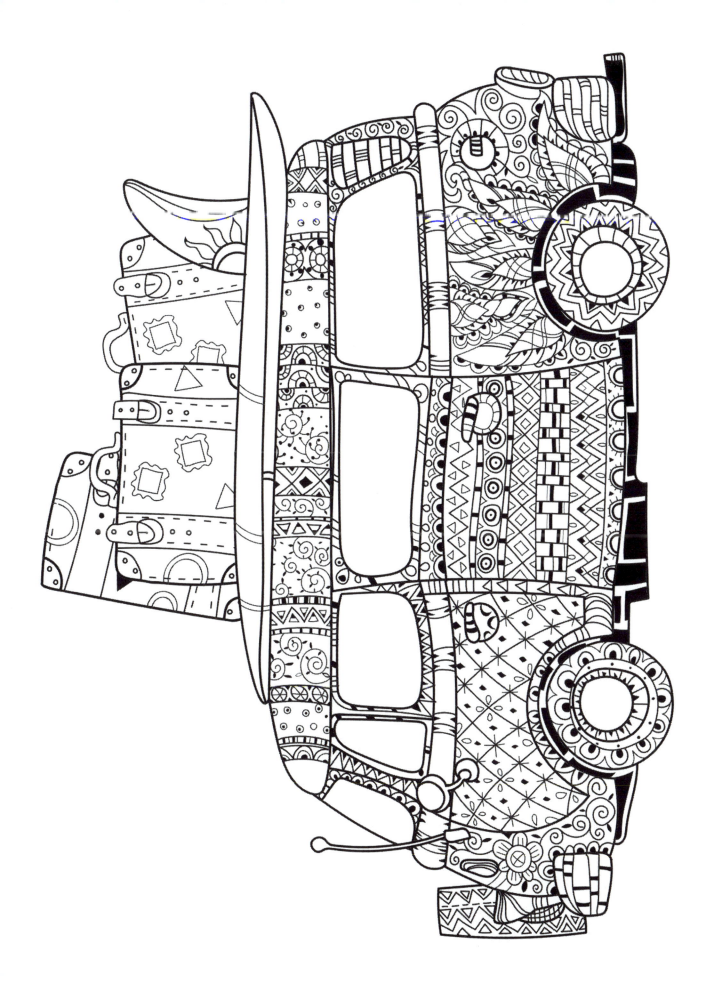

Made in United States
Troutdale, OR
11/02/2024